BRANDING: CREATING AN IDENTITY ON THE WEB

SUSAN MEYER

rosen publishing's
rosen central®

New York

Published in 2015 by The Rosen Publishing Group, Inc.
29 East 21st Street, New York, NY 10010

Library of Congress Cataloging-in-Publication Data

Meyer, Susan, 1986– author.
Branding: creating an identity on the web/Susan Meyer.—First edition.
    pages cm.—(Digital and information literacy)
Audience: Grades 5–8.
ISBN 978-1-4777-7647-6 (library bound)—ISBN 978-1-4777-7649-0 (pbk.)—
ISBN 978-1-4777-7650-6 (6-pack)
1. Branding (Marketing)—Juvenile literature. 2. Internet marketing—Juvenile literature.
3. Social media—Juvenile literature. I. Title.
HF5415.1255.M49 2015
658.8'27—dc23
                                                                2013051220

Manufactured in the United States of America

CONTENTS

INTRODUCTION

Creating a brand is an important part of any marketing plan. Most products are not an entirely new idea. Instead they compete against similar products to appeal to consumers. To set themselves apart from competitors, companies must create a unique identity for their product or company. These marketing identities for products are called brands. According to the American Marketing Association (AMA), a brand is defined as anything that sets a seller apart from other sellers of the same product. Items that can make up a company's brand include a name, term or slogan, sign, symbol, or design.

Sometimes a brand is so well known that it becomes synonymous with the product itself. For example, think about what happens when someone gets a paper cut and wants to protect it from infection. The person might ask someone to bring him or her a Band-Aid. However, "Band-Aid" is actually a brand of adhesive bandage strips. Many other companies also make similar bandages but without a catchy name that people remember. The goal of a good brand is to give a product an identity. Customers will remember this brand identity when they are in the store. Marketers hope that the customer will choose their product over similar products because they connect with the brand.

Another good example of a brand that has successfully owned its marketplace is Google. Founded in 1998 as an Internet search engine,

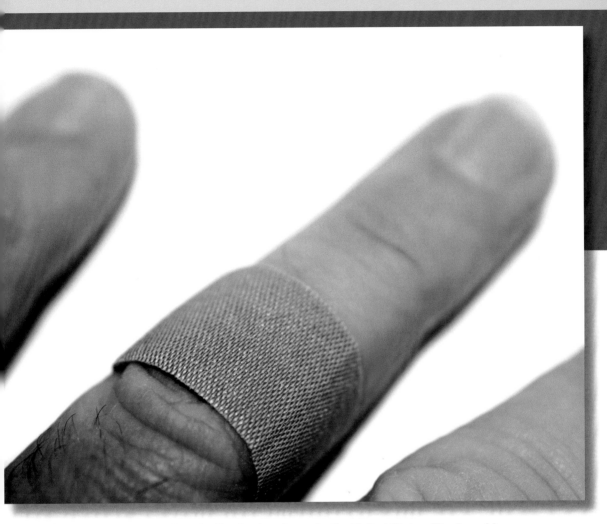

Band-Aid is the largest seller of adhesive bandages in the United States. The brand is so popular that "Band-Aid" is now how people refer to any generic adhesive bandage.

Google.com is, as of 2013, the most frequently visited website in the world. The company Google now controls a search engine; browser; operating system; hardware, including a laptop and tablet; and many specialized add-ons, such as Google Maps, Google Earth, and Google Drive (for creating and storing documents on the web). Much of Google's success and value is in its brand. The company has a clean look and a well-known logo with quirky additions, like changing daily to reflect current events or moments in history. The Google name is so common that in 2006, the word "google" was added to *Merriam-Webster's Dictionary* to describe "searching for information about (someone or something) on the Internet." Google's rock-solid brand marketing has enabled it to dominate every industry it has entered because customers have confidence in the Google brand.

Thirty years ago, brand marketing might have appeared just on bill-boards, in magazine or newspaper advertisements, or on television. Anywhere customers could be reached, a company could spread its slogan, icons, and advertising messages to further its brand. Today, however, digital branding and creating a strong web presence are increasingly important for businesses. A 2011 Pew Research survey found that the Internet, including search engines and social media, are where people get the most information about restaurants and local businesses. Most major businesses also have Facebook pages and Twitter accounts to connect with customers. This relatively new extension of brand identity has brought new opportunities and challenges as customers figure out how to best explore these avenues while staying true to their brand.

While the elements of branding can create a unique identity for a new business, one can also use branding to create one's own identity on the web. Creating a personal brand can be just as important as creating a company's brand. By following a few steps and learning what to say and what not to say, a savvy marketer can get the most out of digital advertising with a truly memorable personal and business identity.

Chapter 1

Branding Basics

The word "brand" originally comes from the Norse word *brandr*, meaning "fire." This referred to the practice of burning a symbol onto a product to mark it. The word "brand" can also refer to marking cattle with a hot iron so that each farmer knows which cows belong to whom. In both cases, the word means separating ownership of a product by some sort of symbol. Today, branding goes far beyond a simple symbol. A company's brand not only includes its slogans, icons, and logos, but also everything it does.

The Value of a Brand

A good brand concept does several things. First, it makes the company's message clear and cements its credibility. People want to buy a product with a proven record, and a good brand can provide that, especially if it has been around for a long time. Second, a brand can get an emotional response from consumers. Research shows that customers are more likely to choose products that they have an emotional attachment to, even when there are similar products that perform the same function. Finally, a brand can

Branding is everywhere, from billboards and magazines to products' boxes and cans. Branding is so common that it can sometimes blend into the background, but its absence is very obvious.

motivate the buyer to make the purchase and cement customer loyalty in the future. Let's say a person sees an ad for a new soda called FrankenDrink and likes the logo of a silly monster on the can. The next time that the consumer sees FrankenDrink on the store shelf, he might buy one. Assuming he likes the product, the next time that he sees a FrankenDrink ad or a can of the drink, he will have a positive association with it. He may buy it again, even though it tastes very similar to his previous favorite soda brand.

A company's brand is often called an intangible asset. An asset is anything that a company owns that has value. These assets include physical items such as warehouses the company owns, the products it sells, and the money it earns. Brand identity can be just as important as these physical assets. A good brand can cause customers to remember the product when they go shopping and prefer one product to another. Brand loyalty is something that all companies seek to gain from customers by putting millions, sometimes billions, of dollars into marketing their brand.

File   Edit   View   Favorites   Tools   Help

BRANDING THROUGH THE AGES

Branding Through the Ages

Today, people get a lot of information about products online. The idea of branding has certainly evolved over the years. It may go back even further than most people realize. Some of the earliest evidence of branding has been found in ancient civilizations. The ancient Babylonians would shout out slogans to encourage customers to buy their spices and carpets over those of other merchants. In ancient Egypt and Rome, store owners painted signs to let customers know what they were selling. They used images instead of words because most of their customers were not able to read, creating the first logos.

In the Middle Ages, makers of many products formed groups to sell their merchandise; these groups were called craft guilds. These guilds each had their own marks and logos. They used town criers to spread the word about their products. They carved wooden signs to represent both the guild and the product. Advanced branding was also seen in China around this time. During the Sung Dynasty, Chinese merchants used the new invention of paper to advertise their products on paper lanterns, banners, and printed leaflets.

Case Studies in Brand Success

Before creating a brand, a company must consider its strengths and weaknesses. What sets it apart from its competitors should be the foundation of the brand. It must focus on its message, its vision, and what its product will stand for. Consider the case study of Nike. Nike creates shoes and other athletic gear, but that isn't the only association that customers make with the

Nike is an official sponsor of the U.S. men's soccer team. The team members wear Nike gear when practicing and playing matches. This gains more exposure for the Nike brand.

Nike brand. The name "Nike" comes from the name of the Greek goddess for victory. Over the years, the company has built up a valuable brand with great recognition among customers. The trademark "swoosh" and the slogan "Just do it" have been around since the 1970s. Nike creates ads that show famous athletes running, jumping, and flipping to victory. All these brand attributes work together to present Nike as a company that sells products that help people achieve and succeed. As of 2010, Nike had one of the most valuable brands among sports merchandisers. In fact, Nike's brand alone is valued at $10.7 billion. This is known as brand valuation.

Apple, the multinational computer company, is another business with a powerful and valuable brand name. Its simple apple silhouette logo and clean, sleek advertisements work together to create a brand that presents itself as both simple and innovative. Apple's branding seeks a very specific audience. The company appeals to the young, hip, and urban. The company differentiated itself from its rival Microsoft in a series of ads in which a young man played an Apple Mac computer and a middle-aged man in glasses played the Microsoft personal computer. These ads had a very clear message: Macs are cool, and personal computers are outdated. This message is Apple's way of setting itself apart from its competitors on the market. Through clear advertising and a consistent tone of innovation throughout its marketing campaigns, Apple has, as of September 2013, the most valuable brand in the world, according to Omnicom Group's "Best Global Brands" report.

Social Media Management

Creating a brand identity is important for any business regardless of its size. In addition to businesses, people can also create brands. We will discuss creating a brand for a person in greater detail in chapter 4. Just creating a brand identity, whether for a person, a local business, or even a huge corporation, isn't enough. In today's Internet-driven world, it's important to have an up-to-date online presence as well. This can take the form of a Twitter page

facebook   Search   🔍

Talk on Facebook for Free!

1 Launch Installer   **2** Complete Install   **3** Talk with Friends!

Save the Bobsled installer! and launch the package from your **Downloads** folder.

Click the **continue** button on the Mac installer. After installation, your browser will restart

You will see phones in your Facebook chat list. **Click here** if you are not automatically directed to Facebook.

Click here if the install doesn't automatically start.

Social media sites can offer a number of helpful communication tools for businesses. The T-Mobile application for Facebook called bobsled allows users to make free phone calls to their friends.

that provides updates on what the company is doing or contests that it might have. Facebook pages can also be used to put out this information as well as photos of a company's products. Both of these sites are social networks. This means that not only can the company post messages that go along with its brand, but fans of the company can comment as well. This gives consumers a place to address anything they like or don't like about what the company is doing or selling. The advantage of this feedback is that it also gives the company a way to respond to customer satisfaction and dissatisfaction directly.

As branding has evolved into the digital age, it has created a recent surge in new careers that have evolved just to meet this need. Many companies now hire people just to handle their social media interaction. Social media managers must understand trends and how to reach people and build a following on social media platforms such as Pinterest, Facebook, Twitter, and YouTube. They must know how to maintain the voice and tone of the brand at all times.

TEN GREAT QUESTIONS
TO ASK A SOCIAL MEDIA SPECIALIST

1   What should I highlight about my business?

2   How do I set my brand apart from my competitors'?

3   Which social media channels would best reach my business's customers?

4   Are there any social media sites that I should avoid?

5   How often should I update my business's social media accounts?

6   What type of content will best engage my customer base?

7   What strategies can I employ to build and increase my business's online following?

8   How quickly should I respond to messages and posts from customers?

9   What is the best way to address criticism in a public forum?

10   Is there anything I should never post on a business social network?

Chapter 2

Finding a Unique Brand

Any new digital business needs a strong brand identity, as discussed in the previous chapter. The brand can set a business apart from businesses offering a similar product or service. Before designing a logo or website, it is important for the business owners to figure out how they would like to represent their company. They must think about what they are trying to sell. Are they trying to advertise their band? Do they have a product, such as handmade jewelry, or even a digital product, such as an app they designed? Are they offering a valuable service, such as mowing lawns or babysitting? All of these businesses can benefit from branding. The first thing to consider when trying to promote or sell something is what makes the product stand apart from similar items or services offered by other businesses. If someone is a babysitter, perhaps he or she wants to focus on his or her many CPR certifications. This could be reflected in the name of the business, the "Safety Sitter," and in the matching logo. Or perhaps the focus of the babysitting business is the sitter's ability to entertain children with magic tricks and juggling skills. The logo of this business could show a happy cartoon clown.

Regardless of what a business is making—be it crafts like jewelry, a new tablet application, or a garage band—all businesses can benefit from marketing and a clear, consistent brand identity.

There is no right or wrong way to brand a company, provided the brand message is consistent. A good marketer should consider the tone that he or she wants to achieve. What associations should consumers make with the business? It could be that the business and its owners are very friendly and easygoing. It could be that they're edgy and use the most up-to-date technology. It could also be that they're very industrious and will work very hard. For business owners who aren't sure what sets their business apart, it's a good idea to try researching local competitors. They can consider what subtle messages they are sending in their own branding. Then they can consider how their product or service can stand out from the crowd. Once they have the message that they would like their business to communicate to customers, it's important for all aspects of their brand—from the logo to the website—to support that message. Branding is best when it is simple and easy to understand. Trying to tell customers too much at once will only be confusing.

Logo Logistics

Once a company has the idea that it wants to convey through its brand, it's time to work on the different elements that will get the brand's message across. It isn't necessary to have all of these things, but each can contribute to the brand. Some suggestions are a logo, slogan, and website.

Starting with the logo, the first thing for business owners to consider is how they can get the brand's message across through an image. A logo is a visual representation of a business and its brand. A good logo should be simple and memorable. Think of McDonald's and its "golden arches" or Nike's special "swoosh." These images are not complicated. They are easy for customers to remember, and when people see these logos, they have an immediate association with the brand. A logo is often placed throughout a company's marketing. It may be included on its signage (if it has a store-front), website and social networks, business cards, stationary, letters, and e-mail sent to customers. It is the first impression that customers may have of the business, so it should be sharp and polished.

Created in 1886, Coca-Cola's logo is the company name written in a Spenserian script. It was tweaked slightly over the years but remains one of the world's most recognizable logos.

There are three main types of logos to consider. The first is a text-based logo. The chosen font or the way the text is arranged is what sets this logo apart. A good example is the particular cursive font of the Coca-Cola logo. It's simple but recognized instantly around the world. The second type of logo is one that illustrates what the company actually does or its name. For example, the logo for the computer company Apple is a silhouette of an apple. The final type of logo is an image that doesn't immediately relate to the name or function of the business. Instead, it becomes associated with it over time. The logo for the popular

Be creative. A logo can be designed using almost any medium. However, it is important to consider how a logo will look on products, websites, business cards, and advertisements.

coffeehouse chain Starbucks is a mermaid with two tails. This image has nothing to do with serving coffee, but it has become one of the most recognizable logos worldwide. Achieving brand recognition for this last type of logo can take many years and cost a lot of money. For a business just getting off the ground, it may be wiser to choose a text-based or literal logo.

After choosing which type of logo they believe would work best for their business, the owners should make rough sketches of how they would like it to look. It's important for it to reflect their brand's message.

File   Edit   View   Favorites   Tools   Help

ELEMENTEO

Elementeo

When Anshul Samar was thirteen years old, he came up with the idea to make chemistry and learning about the periodic table more fun. He created a card game called Elementeo that made the different elements into characters, such as Phosphorous Phoenix. He made the first versions of the game in 2009 by printing them at a FedEx Kinkos. He sold them on Amazon.com and select stores, such as the gift shop at the Exploratorium, a popular science museum.

In 2012, Anshul launched an app version of his game. This new version had features such as being able to play in 3-D and allowing users to make their own Elementeo characters. In launching the new product, he made the announcement on TED Talks, a well-known conference and podcast. He also manages a website for the game and a Twitter account with news on Elementeo.

Launching a successful digital business as a teenager isn't always easy, but Anshul was able to do it by using inexpensive digital marketing. His brand focuses on being educational but also fun. He sought out an audience early on at places such as science museums and has now found new success online by expressing himself intelligently across multiple platforms from social networks to podcasts.

The logo should feature both the name of the company or product and the quality about the company or product that they would like to highlight. After they have a clear idea of what they would like the logo to look like, it's time to create it digitally. Using a scanner, it's possible to create a digital image file or a hand-drawn logo. Another option for logo designers is to recreate their sketches from scratch on a computer. There are special software programs that make logo designing simple through step-by-step instructions and tutorials, such as Logomaker, Laughingbird's Logo Studio, and LogoYes. Some programs have to be downloaded. Young business owners should make sure to research the terms of use and talk to a parent before downloading any programs and especially before buying one.

A Website for Every Business

Once a business has its logo or slogan, it can begin advertising on the Internet. Today, advertising on the Internet is usually the best way to get information about a business and brand out to a lot of people for just a little money. There are a number of different ways to present a brand online. First of all, a website can be created specifically to market the business. For business owners who don't know much about web design, there are many sites that can be used that offer easy templates that can be customized to the business's brand. Sites like Wix.com and Web.com offer a free place to host a website and numerous templates to choose from. A business's website should include its logo and any slogan or brand language that it has developed. It should prominently feature the business's name and give customers a way to contact the business. If the business is being operated out of a young business owner's home, it's not a good idea to give the home's address or phone number for safety and privacy reasons. Instead, the young business owner can set up an e-mail address just for e-mail messages for the business. He or she should make sure this e-mail address has a secure password. Because customers may send personal information over it, the e-mail will need to be kept private.

In addition to creating a website, a business can launch pages on social media platforms, such as Facebook or Twitter. There are a number of social media sites for a business to consider. It must focus on what best advertises its brand or product well. If its product or service is best seen through video casts, it might want to create a YouTube account for the

Launched in 2010, Instagram (as of January 2014) has over 150 million active users around the world. This social media site is great for sharing visual information with customers.

business. If the business is best displayed through photos, it should consider Pinterest or Instagram. A smart marketer does research before creating any accounts for his or her business to make sure that they will add to the brand and complement what the business is trying to sell. As with all aspects of branding, less is often more. Trying to say something too much or in too many different ways can confuse customers and make it difficult to keep sight of the brand's identity.

MYTHS & FACTS

MYTH Creating a valuable product or service will automatically make a new business successful.

FACT Creating a good product is obviously an important part of any business's success, but if customers haven't heard of it, the quality of the product won't be much use. For a business just starting out, the branding needs to give people a reason to give the product a chance. A good brand, thorough marketing campaign, and even incentives, such as new customer offers and deals, will go a long way toward getting the business the recognition for quality that it deserves.

MYTH The more money spent on advertising, the more successful the business will be at getting its brand recognized.

FACT Big businesses may spend billions of dollars on marketing each year, but getting a brand out there doesn't necessarily require a huge budget. By being creative and resourceful and using free methods of advertising online through forums, message boards, and blogs, business owners can drum up interest in their business by spending more time than money.

MYTH The marketing message needs to be changed often to keep things fresh.

FACT Business owners should update their online content regularly, but the overall message should stay the same. The message is the foundation of the brand. Changing this message frequently will confuse customers and make it difficult to see what the company really stands for.

Chapter 3

Cementing a Brand Following

nce a business has created a clear brand, the real work is just beginning. The value of a brand rests on how widely it is recognized by the business's target customers. If people don't recognize or have positive associations with a brand, then that brand is meaningless. Building a strong and valuable brand doesn't happen overnight. It takes a lot of time and effort to get a brand out there.

Once a business has created a website or social networking page as outlined in the previous chapter, it now must begin the task of gathering followers. In order to build the brand, it must encourage people to visit the site and become familiar with what the business does. It also must work to keep current customers happy. Both of these tasks require a time investment. Creating a stylish website, Facebook page, Twitter feed, Pinterest page, or blog is of no use to a brand if it isn't updated regularly and no effort is made to get the word out. A business doesn't want people to visit its sites and find that the information is out of date or that the sites seem abandoned. It might seem appealing to try to reach people on a number of different fronts and launch a brand on five different social networks all at once. However, for

Creating a website and social media pages is not enough. A good business owner puts a lot of time and energy into maintaining these sites and encouraging new followers.

businesses that are just starting out and have a limited amount of time, it's better to start small. They might have a lot of cool ideas for videos about their product to post on YouTube or blog posts to write, but unless they actually have the time to launch these ideas and update them regularly, they may be biting off more than they can chew. New businesses should pick one or two networks that they know they can maintain and use those to build traction with customers.

Customers benefit from social media interaction with businesses. They can voice complaints and share positive feedback. Customers who feel like they are being heard are happier customers.

Creating Traffic

On the road, heavy traffic is something to avoid. However, creating web traffic, or the number of people visiting a site, is exactly what a business wants. There are many ways that a business owner can spread the word and encourage people to visit a site. One of the advantages, from a marketing standpoint, of working digitally is that everyone who uses the Internet is constantly having information gathered about them. Think about the information you yourself have put online. If you have a personal Facebook profile or Twitter feed, you've likely shared information such as your name, gender, and age, as well as some of your interests. In fact, many sites require this information just to sign up. Next time you're on a social network or even when you are using e-mail, check to see what types of advertisements appear in the sidebars for you. Do they seem as if they are directed specifically to teens? Many will also be directed specifically to teens of your gender. websites such as Google and Facebook use the information they collect about you to sell ads to businesses. This is called direct marketing. It enables businesses to target their exact audience.

Businesses can use direct marketing to their advantage. Often websites that sell advertising will charge by the click. This means that if no one clicks on an ad to be taken to a business's website, that business will not be charged for it. If a business doesn't have a budget for marketing, there are still ways that it can find its target audience. It can search for groups of people who might be potential customers. For example, if the business provides a local service such as babysitting or a band that plays gigs around town, it might look for community centers, churches, libraries, or town government websites and groups that it can mention its site to. If these organizations have a Twitter account, a smart marketer can follow them using his or her own business Twitter account. If these local groups have an online message board, a business owner can post on it and introduce himself or herself. Similarly, if a business is selling a product online, such as an app, it can post on message boards in online communities that may be interested in it. The Internet is great at connecting people. The key for

Providing coupons and special offers can encourage new customers to try a product. Discounts for repeat customers who follow a business's social media will help cement a loyal following.

businesses is to focus on just those people who might want their product or service.

Another way for businesses to increase traffic to their sites is to organize promotions and special offers to entice new customers to visit. If their product is digital, such as an app, they might consider offering a free trial version with limited features. Or if they offer a service, they might offer a discount to first-time customers. Putting coupon codes or special offers on social networks and websites will encourage site traffic. People will want to keep checking back in case there are new offers or deals. Businesses can also create

File   Edit   View   Favorites   Tools   Help

TIPS TO KEEP YOUR SOCIAL MEDIA POPPING

Tips to Keep Your Social Media Popping

A. Tang works as a social media manager at a company specializing in gourmet, handcrafted popcorn. She offers some helpful advice for marketing a new digital business on social media:

- Always focus on core brand values, and speak with one voice across all social media platforms.
- Only open social media platforms when you know you have the resources to maintain the energy. It's worse to have a social media channel open that you can't manage.
- Respond in a timely manner. Use appropriate brand language at all times.
- Plan ahead. It's critical to have a good social media plan for all channels. Plan to create content that's relevant, meaningful, and interesting to your specific market.
- Know your target demographic. What are they interested in? What kinds of things do they follow? Who do they talk to and what do they talk about? That's where your content wants to be.
- Be consistent and persistent. Building a social media presence takes time and patience. Keep at it, record your successes and failures, and eventually you'll find your sweet spot.

customer loyalty by offering special deals to people who follow them on Twitter or like them on Facebook. By providing deals and coupons to loyal followers, they provide a greater incentive for loyalty to their brand.

Another option for businesses hoping to reach their target audiences online and spread the word about their sites is to reach out to bloggers who write on a topic related to their business. For example, a jewelry-making business could reach out to fashion bloggers and offer them a free piece of jewelry if they would review it for their readers. The jewelry business could also ask them to advertise a contest on their blogs so that a reader could receive a free product. This situation benefits the blogger, who wants to increase traffic to his or her own site by such contests and promotions, but it will also increase interest in the jewelry business by providing a place to reach potential new customers.

The Customer Is Always Right

A business may have developed a social network or website that is receiving a fair amount of traffic, but it's not done yet. While creating a strong brand

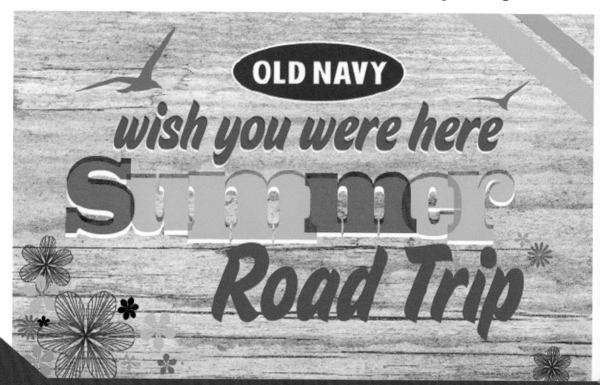

Here is an example of a company providing marketing content that is timely and relevant. The clothing company Old Navy posted this ad in the summer to connect with customers.

requires interest from a lot of people, getting them to continue to check into a business's sites to read the newest updates requires the business to continue to keep content fresh. The voice it uses in all of its customer relations online should echo the brand. For example, if the message of the brand is playful and fun, it should make sure that all of its updates and responses to customers display that.

Response time is important. If a customer posts on a business's Facebook wall, tweets to the business, or writes a review of its product on Yelp or in an app forum, it's important for the business to respond quickly and politely regardless of whether the comment is positive or negative. If a customer comment is a criticism of the business or product, then the business should be apologetic and not defensive. Good customer service is important because it shows customers that the company values their feedback. Another way for businesses to show customers and followers that they appreciate their opinions is to encourage interaction. They can ask questions of their followers to help create a conversation. They can even ask for feedback about their product or service. They can also encourage their customer base to make suggestions. Crowdsourcing ideas from customers is a good way for a business to develop a product in ways it knows its customers will appreciate. As a bonus, when customers feel listened to, they are more likely to be loyal to the brand.

Chapter 4

What's Your Personal Brand?

As mentioned in chapter 1, it isn't just businesses that can be branded. People can be branded, too. In fact, whether they realize it or not, most people are already representing their personal brand online. For everyone who has a web presence at all, they are already putting out messages online that will give people an idea of who they are and what their message is. Take a minute to look through your online profiles. If you have a Facebook, Twitter, Instagram, Tumblr, or Vimeo account, look at both your profile and the communications you have made over these networks. It's also a good idea to use a search engine such as Google to search your name and see what turns up. Think about what each piece of information that you or others have released says about you. Pretend that you're reading the words of a stranger. What would you think about this person? Do they come off as funny? Curious? Rude? A hard worker?

Once you have formed an opinion about how you present yourself online, consider if this is how you would like others to see you. Self-branding

Sharing personal accomplishments online and creating a positive digital footprint is an excellent use of social media resources. Use the Internet to help sculpt your personal brand.

is slightly different from branding a product or business. When branding a business, the business owners are speaking to potential customers of their product. When creating a personal brand, or personal branding, the individual is speaking to everyone. When interacting with friends on the Internet and through social networks, teens can feel like just their friends and classmates will bother to read what they write. That isn't necessarily true.

The Truth Is in the Numbers

According to a survey by the Social Media Research Project at the University of Massachusetts, 22 percent of college admission counselors say they have

Research shows that a person's online presence does affect his future college, internship, and job prospects. Creating a strong personal brand now is investing in one's future self.

looked up a student applicant on a social network. Of these, 12 percent said they saw something a student had posted that negatively affected the student's admission status. The type of posts that most negatively affected admission were those showing students drinking or partying, photos of students doing something illegal or making poor choices, and student posts with offensive language. Also, it isn't just admission counselors for schools that teens might have applied to, but also college recruiters who use social networks as a way to find applicants to recruit. In fact, according to a Kaplan survey, 80 percent of college recruiters use social networks when deciding whom to recruit.

File   Edit   View   Favorites   Tools   Help

THINK BEFORE YOU TWEET

Think Before You Tweet

Although students' digital footprints can show up to affect their college admissions and job opportunities in the future, some students discovered even more negative consequences to their posts on the social network Twitter. In 2013, a New Jersey high school senior, Yuri Wright, was expelled from his Catholic high school for posting several tweets that his school deemed profane and offensive. Prior to the incident, top colleges had been recruiting Wright for football scholarships. After his expulsion, many schools, including the University of Michigan, stopped calling.

It isn't only students in religious or private schools who can face serious consequences for a single tweet. In 2012, Austin Carroll, a senior at a public high school in Indiana, was expelled for using a bad word in one of his tweets. The school said that Carroll's offensive tweet was made on a school computer, which accounted for his expulsion.

In both cases, nothing the boys posted was targeting anyone specific and the posts did not break any laws. However, the consequences were severe. Students can never be too careful when posting content online.

College recruiters aren't just looking for negative posts that might work against an applicant; they're also looking for positive items that can improve the student's chances.

Shining Up a Digital Footprint

To avoid making a poor impression on adults who might view their profiles, there are some things that students should never post on the Internet. These include photos of themselves in scandalous clothing, photos of themselves doing anything illegal, or photos that might display bad judgment. They should also be careful to not use foul or offensive language or say something inflammatory that might come back to haunt them. It's also important for them to monitor not just what they post but also what their friends post about them. Teens should ask their friends to check with them before tagging them in photos or posts or tweeting to them. Even items that students didn't post could reflect on them if these items show up on their network.

Of course, creating an online brand and a positive digital footprint doesn't just depend on what a person doesn't post but also relies heavily on what they do post. Much of the information provided in the previous chapters about brand strategy can be applied to creating a personal brand, too. A personal brander might not need a logo or slogan, but he or she should

What can you tell about this band from this photo they posted? What sort of music do they probably play based on their instruments, style of dress, and presentation?

still have a consistent message. The first step is to decide what that message is. People must decide which of their accomplishments they want to focus on. The brand should also highlight certain personal characteristics. Like all brands, the message should be clear and unwavering. For example, if a student wants to be seen as a hard worker and focuses his posts on goals that he is trying to accomplish, then he shouldn't undermine that message by tweeting or posting a Facebook status update complaining about how he doesn't want to study for his history test.

The Internet has the potential to be one big résumé of a student's work, interests, and accomplishments. If she's a musician, she can post videos or audio of her music online. If he's an artist or photographer, he can make sure that his portfolio is out there for all to see. If she's dedicated to a particular club or social cause, she can consider writing about this interest in a blog. The more positive information students have about themselves online, the more their digital footprint can become an asset to them.

Overall, whether a person is branding a new business or managing a digital footprint, the importance of maintaining a brand identity cannot be overstated. In the digital world, where information is so easy to spread, taking control of what information is out there and harnessing it is a crucial step to success.

GLOSSARY

app A software application, usually downloaded and used on a mobile device.

blogger A person who maintains an online journal or web log (a blog).

brand The unique identity of a company or person.

brand strategy The marketing plan behind a brand.

brand valuation An estimate of how much a company's brand is worth.

corporation A company or group of people operating as a separate business entity.

crowdsourcing Gaining ideas from a group of people, usually over the Internet.

demographic A particular segment of the general population.

digital footprint The personal information online about a specific person.

direct marketing Advertising to a specific group of people.

incentive Something that motivates someone toward an action.

inflammatory Intending to make people angry or upset.

intangible asset Something of value that cannot be touched.

logo A visual representation of a business and its brand.

marketing campaign A plan for creating interest in a product and communicating to customers.

personal branding The practice of people marketing themselves.

promotion A special offer that helps to market a business or product.

social media Online networks where people interact, such as Facebook, Twitter, and YouTube.

social media manager A person who posts content on social network accounts on behalf of a business.

tagging Connecting a person to a photo or update on a social network.

trademark A legally registered symbol, word, or phrase.

traffic The number of people who visit a website.

undermine To make weaker; damage.

FOR MORE INFORMATION

American Marketing Association (AMA)
311 S. Wacker Drive, Suite 5800
Chicago, IL 60606
(312) 542-9000
Website: http://www.marketingpower.com
Since the early 1900s, the American Marketing Association has con-
    nected marketing professionals from across all specialties and
    industries to collaborate on the newest techniques and technologies
    in the field.

Better Business Bureau (BBB)
National Advertising Division
112 Madison Avenue, 3rd Floor
New York, NY 10016
(703) 276-0100
Website: http://www.bbb.org/us/national-advertising-division
The National Advertising Division, part of the Better Business Bureau,
    reviews nationwide ad campaigns for truthfulness and accuracy. Its
    purpose is to foster public confidence in the honesty of advertising.

Canadian Marketing Association (CMA)
1 Concorde Gate, Suite 607
Don Mills, ON M3C 3N6
Canada
(416) 391-2362
Website: http://www.the-cma.org
This organization supports marketers in all disciplines across Canada's
    major business sectors. Through its programs, the CMA encourages

talented marketers while demonstrating marketing's important role in driving business success.

Canadian Youth Business Foundation (CYBF)
100 Adelaide Street West, Suite 1302
Toronto, ON M5H 1S3
Canada
(866) 646-2922
Website: http://www.cybf.ca
The CYBF provides entrepreneurs ages eighteen to thirty-four with professional advice, business resources, and financial support. It helps with all aspects of developing their businesses and offers business grants with the assistance of the Business Development Bank of Canada.

Mobile Marketing Association (MMA)
P.O. Box 3963
Bellevue, WA 98009-3963
(646) 257-4515
Website: http://www.mmaglobal.com
This nonprofit trade association works to promote, educate, measure, guide, and protect the industry of mobile marketing internationally. Additionally, it publishes a resource for marketers, the *International Journal of Mobile Marketing*.

Youth Business America (YBA)
469 9th Street, Suite 240
Oakland, CA 94607-4041

(510) 444-5511
Website: http://www.youthbusinessamerica.org
Youth Business America is an organization that supports qualified young
entrepreneurs by providing informative resources and the one-on-one
volunteer business mentors.

Websites

Due to the changing nature of Internet links, Rosen Publishing has developed an online list of websites related to the subject of this book. This site is updated regularly. Please use this link to access the list:

http://www.rosenlinks.com/DIL/brand

FOR FURTHER READING

Collier, Mark. *Think Like a Rock Star: How to Create Social Media and Marketing Strategies That Turn Customers into Fans*. New York, NY: McGraw-Hill, 2013.

Evans, Liana. *Social Media Marketing: Strategies for Engaging in Facebook, Twitter, & Other Social Media*. Indianapolis, IN: Que, 2010.

Gratton, Sarah-Jayne. *Follow Me! Creating a Personal Brand with Twitter*. Hoboken, NJ: Wiley, 2012.

Handley, Ann, and C. C. Chapman. *Content Rules: How to Create Killer Blogs, Podcasts, Videos, Ebooks, Webinars, and More*. Hoboken, NJ: Wiley, 2012.

Huba, Jackie. *Monster Loyalty: How Lady Gaga Turns Followers into Fanatics*. New York, NY: Penguin Group, 2013.

Kerpen, Dave. *Likeable Social Media: How to Delight Your Customers, Create an Irresistible Brand, and Be Generally Amazing on Facebook (& Other Social Networks)*. New York, NY: McGraw-Hill, 2011.

Martin, Chuck. *The Third Screen: Marketing to Your Customers in a World Gone Mobile*. Boston, MA: Nicholas Brealey Publishing, 2011.

Miles, Jason G. *Instagram Power: Build Your Brand and Reach More Customers with the Power of Pictures*. New York, NY: McGraw-Hill, 2014.

Morgan, John. *Brand Against the Machine: How to Build Your Brand, Cut Through the Marketing Noise, and Stand Out from the Competition*. Hoboken, NJ: Wiley, 2012.

Pipes, Alan. *How to Design Websites*. London, England: Laurence King, 2011.

Salt, Simon. *Social Location Marketing: Outshining Your Competitors on Foursquare, Gowalla, Yelp, and Other Location Sharing Sites*. Indianapolis, IN: Que, 2011.

Schaefer, Mark W., and Stanford A. Smith. *Born to Blog: Building Your Blog for Personal and Business Success One Post at a Time.* New York, NY: McGraw-Hill, 2013.

Scott, David Meerman. *The New Rules of Marketing & PR: How to Use Social Media, Online Video, Mobile Applications, Blogs, News Releases & Viral Marketing to Reach Buyers Directly.* Hoboken, NJ: Wiley, 2013.

Wheeler, Alina. *Designing Brand Identity: An Essential Guide for the Whole Branding Team.* Hoboken, NJ: Wiley, 2012.

Yacomuzzi, Paula. *Logo Construction: How to Design and Build a Logo.* New York, NY: Harper Design, 2012.

BIBLIOGRAPHY

Barden, Phil. *Decoded: The Science Behind Why We Buy.* Hoboken, NJ: Wiley, 2013.

Barker, Melissa, and Donald I. Barker. *Social Media Marketing: A Strategic Approach.* Mason, OH: Cengage Learning, 2013.

Joseph, Jim. *The Experience Effect for Small Business: Big Brand Results with Small Business Resources.* Cupertino, CA: Happy About, 2012.

Kabani, Sharma. *The Zen of Social Media Marketing: An Easier Way to Build Credibility, Generate Buzz, and Increase Revenue.* Dallas, TX: BenBella Books, 2013.

Kaptuta, Catherine. *Breakthrough Branding: How Smart Entrepreneurs and Intrapreneaurs Transform a Small Idea into a Big Brand.* Boston, MA: Nicholas Brealey Publishing, 2012.

Lashinsky, Adam. *Inside Apple: How America's Most Admired—and Secretive— Company Really Works.* New York, NY: Business Plus, 2012.

Paharia, Rajat. *Loyalty 3.0: How to Revolutionize Customer and Employee Engagement with Big Data and Gamification.* New York, NY: McGraw-Hill, 2013.

Samar, Anshul. "At the Top of His Game." *New York Times*, May 25, 2008. Retrieved November 2013 (http://www.nytimes.com/2008/05/25/jobs/25boss.html).

Wiechert, Michael. *Best Social Media Sites for Marketing Your Business and How to Use Each One.* Seattle, WA: Amazon Digital Services, 2013.

Wuebben, Jon. *Content Is Currency: Developing Powerful Content for Web and Mobile.* Boston, MA: Nicholas Brealey Publishing, 2011.

INDEX

About the Author

Susan Meyer is the author of a number of young adult educational books about integrating new digital resources. Meyer has experience in creating branding for her own business pet projects with the help of her talented graphic designer husband. Meyer currently resides in Queens, New York.

Photo Credits

Cover, p. 1 (from left) © iStockphoto.com/enjoynz; © iStockphoto.com/ljdema; © iStockphoto.com/grandriver; © iStockphoto.com/franckreporter; p. 5 STILLFX/Shutterstock.com; p. 8 Roman Samokhin/Shutterstock.com; p. 10 Victor Decolongon/Getty Images; p. 12 AP Photo/T-Mobile USA; p. 16 Stockbyte/Thinkstock; p. 18 Scott Olson/Getty Images; p. 19 © iStockphoto.com/ bowdenimages; p. 22 Press Association/AP Images; p. 25 Ryan McVay/Photodisc/Thinkstock; p. 26 Dean Drobot/Shutterstock.com; p. 28 Yinyang/E+/Getty Images; p. 30 PRNewsFoto/Old Navy/AP Images; p. 33 William Casey/Shutterstock.com; p. 34 mast3r/Shutterstock.com; pp. 36–37 Roxana Gonzalez/Shutterstock.com; cover (background) and interior page graphics © iStockphoto.com/suprun.

Designer: Nicole Russo; Editor: Heather Moore Niver;
Photo Researcher: Marty Levick